THE

TABERNACLE

OF

DAVID

END TIME REVIVAL

KENNETH M. SMITH

Independently Published-Psallo Press

ISBN 9781954626027

Kenneth M. Smith
4251 E Lakeview Dr
Martinsville, In 46151

Website
www.gloryrealmministries.org

Facebook
www.facebook.com/KenAndDebrahSmith

CONTENTS

DEDICATION

I dedicate this short book to the Lord Jesus Christ who has taken me on a 41 year journey in exploring this subject in the Word of God. I have always related to the main character, David, who was a man after God's own heart. His life story and objective is my inspiration for all my hours of study as a musician to discover the secrets and revelation of the Tabernacle of David.

Thanks to my wife for editing, publishing and sharing this journey as we endeavor to bring God's Presence to others as we publicly worship and praise our Lord and Savior.

CHAPTER ONE

THE TABERNACLE OF DAVID
THE RIVER OF GOD

"In that day I will raise up the fallen tabernacle of David, And wall up it's breaches; I will also raise up it's ruins, And rebuild it as in the days of old; 12 That they may posses the remnant of Edom and all the nations who are called by my Name," Declares the Lord who does this.
13 "Behold the days are coming," declares the Lord, "When the plowman will overtake the reaper and the treader of grapes him who sows seed....
Amos 9:11-13a

Every time I have read this passage of scripture I see a most awesome picture of the power of anointed worship. Worship that is uninhibited and totally surrendered to the move of the Spirit of God, freely flowing like the Holy River from Heaven. The clear crystalline River of Life in the Paradise of God flows through the middle of the

1

Garden, and then flows down into the Earth Realm and into the hearts of believers. Jesus explains,

"Whoever believes in me, as scripture has said, Out of your belly shall flow rivers of living water."(John 7:38). "By this He meant the Spirit, whom those who believed in Him were later to receive. Up to that time the Spirit had not been given, since Jesus had not been glorified."(verse 39)

What a beautiful visualization of the Holy Ghost River of God! It flows through Heaven and then flows down to Earth into the hearts of every believer. On this last and greatest day of the Feast of Booths (Tabernacles), as Jesus was calling out to the thirsty souls, a ceremonial 40 gallon drum of water was poured out over the stone pavement outside of the temple. As this water spilled out, Jesus' cry was heard in the streets by those who thirsted after Him and what he offered them: a real encounter with Heaven's River. The people perceived His authority; much more than the mere ritual offered by the Scribes and Pharisees. Can you begin to see and feel the River? The mist is rising… Jesus' offer is for all of us, and His intention is that we will be filled to overflowing with His Spirit, so that it will pour out onto others, with healing, salvation, and deliverance. All Glory to God!

The overflow is the result of being filled with the Holy Spirit to the point of flowing over. We can contain so much of Him until we are saturated. Then comes a point where we are unable to contain any more and our human vessel can then pour out onto others the powerful Grace of God. The result is the Healing River of God flowing into the hearts of those around us.

There is another place where the scriptures speak of living waters flowing. In Ezekiel 47:1-12 is a picture of water coming forth from under the threshold and the altar of the Temple of the Lord. It flowed in increments as it went; first it was ankle deep, then knee deep, then waist deep and finally so deep that it was enough to swim in, a River of God. Look at verse 12:

"And by the river on it's bank, on one side and on the other, will grow all kinds of trees for food. Their leaves will not wither, and their fruit will not fail. They will bear every month because their water flows from the sanctuary, and their fruit will

be for food and their leaves for healing."

This is a prophetic mirror image of the River of Life in Heaven and the life-giving trees that bear fruit every month for healing.(Revelation 22:1-2) And the river also brought healing and refreshing wherever it flowed; even the dead waters became healed and alive when this water touched them. Your life, through the life-giving flow of the Spirit, will bring life and healing to every dead thing it touches. Death, sickness, sorrow, religion and control gives way to the flow of Heaven. Hallelujah to the Lamb of God!!! Be healed right now in the River flow…

CHAPTER TWO

DAVID THE SWEET PSALMIST OF ISRAEL

Now when you mention the name of David, I think of the sweet Psalmist of Israel. He brought back true Worship to the God's chosen people, Israel, the apple of His Eye. He was God's man. The Father testifies about His son David.

"A man after my heart, who will do all my will."(Acts 13:33)

God provided Himself a King from the sons of Jesse. Young David was around 15 years of age when he stood before Samuel to be anointed with the holy oil. It was another 5 years before David came to the battle front and heard the Philistine giant cursing God. That anointing on his life was what directed a smooth stone which David slung right into the forehead of the giant Goliath. David's declaration of his covenant with God qualified that smooth stone to hit it's mark. The huge Phillistine had no covenant with God and therefore had no standing in this battle. All of his swelling words of pride availed him nothing. The devil's defeat here only depended upon a word of truth from the young man, David. Down Goliath goes with a loud thud as the rock of God's deliverance sinks deep into the giant's forehead. Then David takes Goliath's giant sword and takes off his head! The enemy Phillistine army fled in terror. Even though this demonic leader of the enemy army was over 9 feet tall and covered with armor weighing 150 pounds, he was no match for the anointed covenant man of God.

Now, enter the stage, King David, age 20, a man after God's own heart. Worship was in his DNA, for he had been taken from the sheepfolds, where much time had been spent in Psalmistry, out in the open fields, learning the ways of God. It pleased the Father to promote David, for Saul had no heart for worship. Saul began humbly, hiding in the lost luggage, but quickly lost his way. He was rebuked by God through the prophet Samuel for failing his first test, by not waiting on God's timing, fearing the people and going ahead without consulting God. It is a sad thing when promotion turns people from humility to pride. Saul was not seeking the God of Israel any more, but only the throne of self. Jealousy had set in when he heard the people singing:

"Saul has slain his thousands, and David his tens of thousands" (1 Samuel 18:7)

When he became tormented by an evil spirit, he needed the true anointing on David's life to give him breakthrough and relief. Saul became so backslid that he ended up consulting a witch for wisdom and dying in battle without God or His Presence.

David came along with an anointing to kill the giants, the demonic principalities who ruled the land, in order to restore heavenly worship to God's people. It was Worship which took back the land from the enemy. Notice that he took 'five smooth stones', not because he might miss and need extra ammo, but his mission was to take out all the giants; Goliath had four brothers who also were destroyed by David. The principalities and powers had to be subdued before God's Kingdom reign could be established. His one mission on Earth was to bring back the Ark of the Covenant, the symbol of God's Presence, to Jerusalem. He understood this as bringing God's Presence into the forefront of all society, and so ushered in a reign of Peace on Earth for forty years of his reign. Davidic worship changed the Atmosphere of this time.

The ark of the covenant was carried by the sanctified priests for nine miles from Baalah (Kiriath Jearim) to Jerusalem. In a magnificent procession, David danced before the Lord as it entered the city of Jerusalem. This King's worship was so undignified and abandoned before God that he danced his clothes off. Only his under tunic was left on him as he sweated and celebrated and praised. His wife Michal, Saul's daughter, disdained him in jealousy of the young maidens who were enamored with the King's worship. Here again jealousy of Worship cost her dignity, even though David had lost his dignity. She was struck barren for the rest of her days. This was the ultimate curse and dishonor of a Jewish woman. David ended up with several wives who would honor and worship God. This king's heart for worship caused him to survive all enemies, even his own sin and failure, because God still had his heart. The Father pronounced, 'David's dynasty would never be removed', making him the prototype of the eternal Kingdom of Jesus Christ Himself.

After King David returned the Ark of God to Jerusalem there was an Open Heaven for 33 years. These were prophetic years, the same number of years that Jesus lived on Earth. Jesus on Earth was our open portal to the third Heaven being manifested on Earth. Jesus in every believer's heart today is our open portal to Heaven now! The entire known world was shifted into acknowledgement of the Heavenly Realm of God. The Peace of God reigned supreme in the land.

Worship ushered in by the Breath of God was released upon 288 temple musicians and singers, who carried this sound from Heaven. David's Heavenly Worship Band played their hearts out day and night. They changed players every hour, to bring in a fresh sound and a fresh revelation. Even the night watches were filled with instrumental and vocal release of Heaven's reality, created by music and lyrics. Eventually there were over 4000 temple singers and musicians in David's orchestra.

The Mighty Power of Yahweh was released in the Earth, emanating from it's capitol city, Jerusalem. This geographical place mirrored the song coming from it's heavenly counterpart, the New Jerusalem above, which is free. Glory to God!

After this, his son Solomon would build the magnificent temple of worship. There was a large gap between the time Israel camped around the 'Presence in the Wilderness' with Moses, and the time when David arrives in the timeline. Worship had pretty much been lost as central to Israel's posterity. Dead religion had set in during Saul's reign as the first king. The Ark of His Presence had been relegated to the high places where the mid-week service took place. Kind of reminds me of the modern church. We have reduced worship to a short preliminary before preaching the word. Please notice I used the word, preliminary. Wrong! Worship is the main event opening the way for the Teacher of the Word, the Holy Spirit, to explain what happened in the Worship encounter.

Remember, Israel camped around the Presence. Teaching the word of God is also important, but the Worship is for Him. Teaching is instruction for us. Even so, I contend that we have had so much teaching that we have become fat. Most of us haven't even walked out the knowledge we have already received. This is Greek thinking that everything surrounds more knowledge. Ray Hughes says this about worship:

" When the Throne of God is the center of the church, instead the pulpit, the Presence of God will rule there"

You will notice in the accounts of the good and bad Kings of Israel that the "High Places" were never taken down, even during restoration periods. In the High Places people worshiped a mixture of Jehovah worship combined with customs of worshiping other gods. For there are many gods. Today we have many gods in America. But, the Most High God says, "You will have no other gods before Me".

Worship opens the way for the flow of the Spirit who brings life to the living word. Remember, Israel camped around the Presence of God. The heathen nations trembled when they heard the shout of God coming from Israel's camp! The ground shook and the devil's camp feared the awesome power of the God of Israel. This was David's commission: to restore to God's people, the Presence and the power of Heaven.

The Ark was captured by the Phillistines during Saul's reign and was placed in the temple of Dagon, their god. The statue of Dagon fell down before the Ark and his hands and head were broken off, face down before God at the threshold. This is a picture of the end of all things when "Every knee will bow and every tongue will confess that Jesus Christ is Lord". There is only one ultimate power in the universe! There is a threshold where the sounds of worship drives the devil away. The curse of the emrods (hemorrhoids) came upon the five cities of the Phillistines because of the anointing of God's Presence. God gave them some personal issues they couldn't ignore! Lol. Every day, every believer should be driving the devil crazy and giving him a headache. You know, the devil's crowd doesn't know how to handle the anointing of God. So they sent the Ark away on a new cart, and it arrived back in the land of Israel, pulled by milk cows, lowing as they went. Can you imagine the sight of the Ark of God rolling into Beth-Schemesh on an ox cart? Wow! Here again, God's people did not know how to handle the Presence properly with respect and reverence. Some men looked into the ark and were struck down (50,070). The Law of God is: the Ark without the Mercy Seat is deadly to human flesh. Therefore the levites took it into the house of Abinadab (in the nearby hills) at Kiriath Jearim, and set apart Eleazar, his son to keep the ark of Yahweh.(1 Samuel 7:1)

"It happened, from the day that the ark abode in Kiriath Jearim, that the time was long; for it was twenty years: and all the house of Israel lamented after YAHWEH." I Samuel 7:2

So we see that the innermost yearnings of a worshiping people is for the reality of God to be manifest in our midst. When the ark (Presence) is missing, worship is empty and ritualistic. We need the real Jesus!

This is so amazing to me that this artifact which represented the heart of Worship for the Hebrew race was basically lost for twenty years. It is no wonder that all the house of Israel lamented after their God; they were crying out for leadership to seek out and restore their fortunes. How much does this translate today in our modern church world? The faithful worshipers in the pews really do long for reality and fulfillment in their service to the house of God. The Pastors and leaders are either seeking to please God in these matters of the Kingdom, or be found guilty of building their own kingdoms. The ultimate failure of our leadership is to curry the fear of man and the quest for monetary blessing, rather than receive the blessing of the Kingdom by reverencing the God of Heaven. Our Father pays for every endeavor he calls for. The provision for the vision is already set aside. Therefore Matthew 6:33 reads:

"Seek first the Kingdom of God and His righteousness, and all these other things will be added unto you."

The Father was getting his man ready for 20 years to bring true worship back to His people. Therefore, David's ultimate achievement was to take the Ark of God from it's temporary resting place in the 'field of the woods' (Kiriath Jearim) to the city of Jerusalem, and set it under a thin veil, a tent, in the plain sight of all the people. Worship became the main event before the eyes of all, not hidden in the Holy of Holies for only the high priest to see. The mercy seat was set in public for all to come and give praises and thanksgiving to the one who gives life. The Ark of the covenant was the central piece needed to release the Glory upon the land. It is interesting to note that the furniture created for the Tabernacle, in the wilderness, is designed after the prototype that is in Heaven itself. Everything we see here on Earth is made according to the pattern in Heaven. So even the patterns of Worship are ordained from the things above. Worship effectively changed the entire known world of David's time and rule. It was Heaven's manifestation on Earth. Jesus tells us today that the Father will manifest Himself to us if we are intimately in love with Him, and obedient to Him.

CHAPTER THREE

WHAT IS THE BREACH?

*"I will rebuild the Tabernacle of David
and repair it's breaches." (Amos 9:11b)*

There is a breach between God and His people.
A breach is a break, a broken place, a distance created between two people …between a people and
their God. John the revelator describes it this way:

*…"I have somewhat against you because you have
left your first love.
Remember therefore from where you are fallen,
and repent, and do the first works"…(Revelation
2:4-5a)*

Think back when you first met Jesus, how you
were devoted and spent quality time with Him.
Your worship was pure and simple. Jesus was
speaking to the church at Ephesus, who had become orthodox and doctrinally correct, but lacked
passion. Like the modern church of today, we have

become good at "having church." We have our 3 or 4 songs and a poem, collect our offering and say goodbye till next time. We start at 10:45 and are done by 11:45; But we are not changed. And we don't have the power to change others. This is why the world is not interested in coming to "church." We need Revival.

"Having a form of godliness but denying the power thereof." (11 Timothy 3:5)

How do we just go through the motions and deny the power of the gospel? We cut off the intimacy of our worship. We entertain and keep people engaged with lights and smoke machines and dance, but we lack the purposeful encounter with Holy Spirit. This encounter comes as we spend time and quiet moments expressing our love to God. We are afraid to lose people here as they become uncomfortable and at a loss for words. This culture of worship needs to be birthed and experienced by every person, beyond the mundane, into life-changing exchanges with Him, the One that we are accountable to. Reverently and purposely giving a time and place for Heaven's Reality to set in is a key ingredient lacking in much of what we call worship. These one hour services are more like a laundromat experience, washing and drying our clothes quickly so we can beat the Baptists to the cafeteria. For some, this is their only weekly time set aside for God.

When a time of separation happens, such as right now, God is calling for His true worshippers to be set apart. The sheep are being separated from the goats, the wise virgins are being separated for the five foolish virgins. They all were called of God, but only half survived the test. It bears witness that only a remnant of the church are ready for the first bus out of planet Earth in the rapture, the catching away of the saints (1 Thessalonians 4:17) . If any one misses the intervention of God, who will forcibly snatch away His church in the rapture, he will be left behind to be persecuted by the Anti-Christ. As I am writing this, a separation is occurring, separating the sheep from the goats.

Jesus is going to repair the breach and set our hearts on fire. David cries out:

"Will you not revive us again that your people may rejoice in you?" (Psalm 85:6)

And again:

Your people will volunteer freely in the day of your power; (Psalm 110:3)

Yes Jesus, send us your power! We repent of our lukewarmness, break in upon us, and cause these dry bones to live again…I hear the sound of the dry bones rattling… (lyric by Elevation worship)

CHAPTER FOUR

THE WAR OVER WORSHIP

Here on Earth there is a War over Worship. The rogue cherub who fell from Heaven took one third of the angels with him in his fall. He was the 'covering Cherub' who presided over Worship which covers the Throne in Heaven. Even his body was an instrument that created sounds through his 'pipes and timbrels' (Ezekiel 28:13). This gives us the impression of some sort of a pipe organ accompanied by percussion sounds. Lucifer was lifted up with pride because of his beauty and thought Heaven should worship him instead of his Creator, the Ancient of Days. So you see there was disloyalty even in what we would call a perfect place like Paradise. This upset the order of things in the universe, for now there must also be a place called hell where the devil and his angels must be tormented for eternity. Worship in Heaven was affected by the loss of one third of the worshiping angels, so now God is looking for Worshipers to cover the Throne, because the covering cherub who lost his place in Heaven. The Father is looking for the true Worshippers.(John 4:23) God is Spirit, therefore those who worship Him must worship Him in Spirit and in Truth. Human beings are now brought into this war, to see who they will serve. We can choose to Worship God who is in Heaven, or serve satan. This is why the Father honors loyalty, because even His Kingdom was marred by disloyalty.

Revelation 12:11-13
"And they overcame him because of the blood of the lamb and because of the word of their testimony, and they did not love their life even to death."
12 "For this reason rejoice O heavens and you who dwell in them. Woe to the earth and the sea, because the devil has come down to you having great wrath, knowing that he only has a short time.
13 "And when the dragon saw that he was thrown down to the earth, he persecuted the woman who gave birth to the male child."
17 "And the dragon was enraged with the woman, and went off to make war with the rest of her offspring, who keep the commandments of God and hold to the testimony of Jesus."

DO YOU IDENTIFY YOURSELF IN THIS WAR?

Wasn't this always the issue from the beginning? The devil is enraged with the worshipers of God, because he is jealous and wants it all for himself. He even asked Jesus to bow down and worship him during the temptation in the wilderness. Can you just imagine what Jesus was thinking: "I still remember when I created you in heaven". Satan was so desperate that he offered to give him all the kingdoms of this world if Jesus would just bow down to him. Notice the enemy didn't offer this until Jesus mortal body was weak from fasting for 40 days. Actually the offer was made to by-pass the cross and forfeit buying back the human racc with His blood. Jesus' reply was the first commandment:

"You shall worship the Lord your God, and Him only will you serve."(Luke 4:8)

"You've got to serve somebody. It might be the devil or it might be the Lord, but you've got to serve somebody".(lyrics from Bob Dylan)

The Pharoah of Egypt was another person who

was jealous of the worship of Yahweh. Pharoah would not let God's people go to worship Him. They were his slaves who served in this house of bondage for 400 years. Their song was lost, but their cries came up into the ears of the Lord, their God in Heaven. Moses came and demanded their release, and finally, after God sent His judgments upon the Egyptian households, Pharaoh let them go, and Israel left with all the riches of Egypt (back pay for all their years of service). Even as the Pharoah hardened his heart against them, he then changed his mind and pursued the Hebrews into the Red Sea (the Blood of Jesus) and was drowned with all his army. But as the Israelites crossed over on dry ground to the other side of the sea, they got their song back. Miriam danced and sang with the others, "Pharoah and his chariots are drowned in the midst of the sea." The song of the Lord had been lost for 400 years and was now found again in their hearts of His people. Worship prevailed! Deliverance from bondage became reality.

There is another person who was jealous of Heaven's Worship; King Herod. The Herod family regime had ruled over Israel for generations. Their pride and control were challenged when certain wise men came into town asking 'Where is the child, the King of the Jews? 'We have seen His star in the east'. Word of these seekers came into the ears of Herod and he became very jealous of his throne. There was not room for two Kings in Israel! So this wicked King called for these wise men to appear before him so he could question them concerning when they had first seen this star from the east. These worshippers had traveled 900 miles in pursuit of the star, a two year journey on camel. Herod took note of this and pretended to also be a worshipper of God, so he asked them to bring word when they found the child. Then, calling upon the Jews concerning the prophecies, asked what was written in their scriptures concerning this King. They cited the prophet Micah, chapter 5 verse 2:

"And you Bethlehem, in the land of Judah, are by no means least among the rulers of Judah, for out of you will come a ruler who will shepherd my people Israel."

Learning of the times and seasons and the place of His birth, Herod became angry, and decreed that all male children up to the age of two should be killed. He was sure he had removed his competition for the throne in the land of Palestine...but the wise men went home another way, being warned in a dream not to trust Herod. They came and presented their gifts and worshipped the King of Kings and Lord of all Lords.

Then God further protected the Holy child Jesus by warning his step-father Joseph to hide the child in Egypt. The very gold that was brought as a gift from the magi provided the funds to travel and live for two years until Herod died, so that the holy family could return safely to Israel. For Herod, lifted up in his pride, failed to give the glory to God when the people said, " It is the voice of God and not a man". Herod took the Glory that only belongs to God, so the Bible tells us that he was eaten up of worms. That is the epitaph of a man who was jealous of God's ruler whom He has set to be worshipped. Worship belongs to God alone because of His Worth-ship!

This war still rages on and there is a sifting and a separation between them that serve God And them who serve him not. The gray areas are disappearing and the fence is gone. You cannot ride the fence any longer. Jesus is enlisting you into His army-band. The wise and unwise virgins, the sheep and the goats, the children of light versus children of the darkness. Presently there is a sifting and a shaking in the earth revealing the Sons of God in the midst of a crooked and perverse nation. Do you realize that the Father could snap His finger and this whole saga would be over? But, you see, Adam gave up his authority in the original garden. The second Adam, Jesus, defeated darkness through the cross...

"ALL AUTHORITY HAS BEEN GIVEN TO ME IN HEAVEN AND ON EARTH, GO THEREFORE..."(Matthew 28:18)

We have been given authority to take it back. Until we rise up and take it back, it will remain in satan's hands. I want to inject this word here: this whole war is rigged in our favor. There is no way that satan can win this conflict. This battle is rigged in our favor! God is causing us to crush satan under our feet. All we have to do is not quit. We win hands down! At the time of this writing, the church is being awakened to bring in the final billion soul harvest; This is what Jesus died for and we are going to see it happen because the move has begun! The wearing of masks and social distancing are satan's weapons. Welcome to the war! Worship is our warfare, our Praise is a weapon!!! THIS WAR WE DO WIN!!!

Just begin to shout HALLELUJAH!!!

CHAPTER FIVE

THE TABERNACLE TODAY

What does the Tabernacle of David mean to the world we now live in?

The restoration of the Tabernacle of David is an end times event predicted in the prophecy of Amos 9:11:

"In that day I will raise up (again) the fallen Tabernacle of David..."

God raised it up first through the heart of His servant David, but in these last days He will raise it up again through the hearts of His Worshiping Army Bride.

So why does this tabernacle need to be raised up? Glad you asked. The short answer is so that the entire human race can be saved. Of course, not everyone will respond to the invitation. Remember, it is God's will that every person come to repentance, that none would perish and all would receive everlasting life. In the book of Acts chapter 15:16-17 James (the Lord's brother) is quoting Amos 9:11-13 as an explanation of the move of Holy Spirit proceeding from the day of Pentecost. The prophecy is stated with a new insight:

16 "After these things I will return,
And I will rebuild the Tabernacle of David
which has fallen, And I will rebuild it's ruins, And I
will restore it,
17 In order that the rest of mankind may seek the
Lord, and all the gentiles who are called by My
name.

This interpretation of the original verse adds the evangelistic emphasis in verse 17. This means that Tabernacle worship will be the catalyst for end-time revival. Worship opens the door for kingdom power to be released. Encountering Jesus in His Power is what caused the Jerusalem council to address this huge gentile harvest coming in to the Kingdom of God. This old testament promise of rebuilding David's Tent was given new relevance pertaining to the last days which began after Jesus resurrection. We are now entering the end of the age and the "beginning of sorrows" referred to by Jesus in Matthew 24:8. These sorrows include the spirit of anti-Christ being prevalent, wars and rumors of wars, nation rising against nation, kingdom against kingdom, famines, pestilences and earthquakes. The covid-19 pandemic is a great pestilence upon us. The frequency of earthquakes in various locations and intensity portrays the picture of a mother getting ready to give birth, as the birth pangs reach fever pitch just before the delivery. The Kingdom is preparing to give birth to the manifestation of the Son's of God. All creation is crying out for deliverance. We are all on God's operating table and the inevitable is upon us. Jesus will not return until the Father grants him his greatest prize; the entire Harvest that must come in before the end. Yes, that means China, Europe and the Middle East! Jesus did not give His life for any thing less than the full end-times Harvest of Souls. Only after the last Harvest does Jesus say, "Then shall the end come" (Matt.24:14)

Multiplied Harvest

Amos 9:13

"Behold the days are coming," declares the Lord, "When the plowman will overtake the reaper and the treader of grapes him who sows seed....

Can you see the picture here. The plowman is the guy who drops his plow blade in the ground and gets the soil ready for new seed. Soil in scripture represents men's hearts. The heart is where we have faith and receive from God every good thing. The seed is the incorruptible Word of God. The secd is always 100 percent viable and ready to produce. The ground, or soil, is always the unknown factor when it comes to harvest. Only the good ground produces 100-fold. The first three soil types, (the wayside, the rocky soil and the thorny ground) have a complete crop failure every time the Word is preached! That means that only 25 percent of the seed sown bears fruitful harvest. As stated in Mark 4:20:

"And those are the ones on whom seed was sown on the good soil; and they hear the word of God and accept it, and bear fruit, thirty, sixty and a hundredfold."

The 100-fold would account for only about 8 percent of the church (25 percent divided by 3). What can God do with 8 percent? Turn the world upside down as the early Apostles of Jesus did! So, you see, in the final Harvest the plowman is getting the soil ready for another crop, and the reaper is trying to hurry up and get out of his way, because this is a bumper crop. The harvest is going to be so great that sowing and reaping will almost become simultaneous.

Our heavenly Father is desiring the main ingredient: true worship, even as Jesus spoke about to the woman at the well in Samaria. Remember Jesus said, "I must go through Samaria." Jesus went out of His way to encounter this woman who was seeking the truth. He also knew that revival would break out in that city because of the hungry heart of one infamous lady who would testify to her people about a miraculous encounter with God. This is the kind of worshipers the Father is seeking, they that will worship Him in Spirit and in truth. Because the Father is a Spirit, they that worship Him must worship Him in Spirit, and therefore, in Truth. Jesus said there would be a day coming in which this would happen.

This Samaritan woman represents a huge part of the final harvest that Jesus is looking for. Jesus stated:

"I must go through Samaria." (John 4:4)

These were an unreached people group because they were a half-breed race, Jews who had intermarried with other races. And this woman was in need of forgiveness for her life-style of one relationship after another. She represents the modern church. We are provoking the jealousy of Father-God by having illicit love affairs with the world of idols. Sounds like today doesn't it? Sin is rarely addressed in todays seeker-sensitive churches. People come in feeling comfortable to shack up and sit in the middle row of the congregation. Social drinking is totally acceptable. You can't tell a Christian from a non-believer. Since lifestyle is not preached, there is no conviction for sin. We treat having a relationship with God casually. Lastly, these people had false claims to son-ship simply because they were relatives of the Patriarch Jacob. Americans feel like they are right with God simply because they live here in this country and have some relative who knew God. The Samaritans had false religion and needed to be brought into the true vine, Jesus the Messiah. America needs to repent and fall in love with Jesus again.

The woman of Samaria went out to evangelize the entire city after one encounter with the real Jesus. How much more will this present generation do to proclaim that "Jesus Christ is the answer", so that the world will see true Christianity in you and I ? These were her words of testimony:

"Come and see a man who told me all the things I have done" (John 4:39b)

In that same verse we see that many believed in Jesus because of these words of this converted woman. Her character was so altered that belief was sparked by her simple testimony of Jesus. People came out to see what had caused this miracle.

The story doesn't end here. These Samaritan people asked Jesus to stay with them. He stayed for 2 days. This represents 2000 years of the gentile season of Harvest we are in now, and approaching the end of the second thousand years or, second day, before Jesus returns to take us home. Now hear the testimony of these ones as they hear Jesus voice for themselves:

"It is no longer because of what you said that we believe, for we have heard for our selves and know this One is indeed the savior of the world" (verse 42)

You see, our testimony can bring them in, but discipling them to hear Jesus for themselves will create an unstoppable army of God! What a contrast to the insipid, status quo church of today, that Jesus calls lukewarm. This is why He tells us to repent and do the things we did at the first (first love), or else He will remove our candlestick from it's place. This is also a stark reality as I write these words. The light in many has been extinguished. But the Fire of God is baptizing another remnant group who will usher in the final Harvest through heart-felt and fiery Worship of the One whom our soul loves.

So you see here a representation of the last billion-soul harvest prophesied about by many. China, the Middle East and much of Europe must come in before our job is done. A large number of these will be young people. I have heard from the Spirit that Jesus will raise up children to get the job done if He can't get cooperation from the adults. Are you hearing His Voice? Jesus is tired of lukewarmness. In China it is reported that the underground church is growing exponentially, largely spearheaded by 14 to 19 year olds going from village to village in rural areas, starting house churches. These are then turned over to older converts while the youth keep moving on preaching Jesus. In Iran Jesus Himself is appearing to the lost souls of the Arab world. Listen to the warning of Jesus:

"So then, because you are lukewarm, and neither hot nor cold, I will spit you out of my mouth."
Revelation 3:16

The Lord of Heaven tells us that even being cold to Him is better than being halfway, trying to ride the white fence between Heaven and Earth. People mill around there to see how close to the world they can remain and still make it into Heaven. Jesus says this is not what He died for. The Master desires us to give up ourselves to Him and encounter the Holy Fire of God that consumes all impurities. The very fire from the Holy Altar of God in the midst of the Throne coming from the sapphire stones of Fire…(Exodus 24:10). The Throne itself is being lifted up by the Seraphim crying out night and day, "Holy, Holy, Holy!" These are the ones who carry the Glory and Revival fire that brings in the Great Harvest. People are hungry in light of the void we are experiencing, and only the REAL JESUS will be able to capture the hearts of these ripe souls. People around us must feel the Love and compassion of the Savior. Religion has no draw. Man's imitation of the real has no power to save. The sleeping giant of Praise and Worship of a Holy people is awakening to lift her hand as the dawning of a new day which is on the horizon. Can't you see it and begin to feel it now?

CHAPTER 6

HARP AND BOWL WORSHIP

In these intense and troubled times in which we live, the Holy Spirit of God is raising up a powerful force in the Earth; that is the fuel which burns bright during the darkest hours of the night.

"Arise, shine; for your light has come , and the Glory of the Lord has risen upon you.
For behold, darkness will cover the earth, and deep darkness the peoples; but the Lord will rise upon you, and His glory will appear upon you."
(Isaiah 60: 1-2)

This day was predicted and will become the church's finest hour. I know it doesn't look like it, but the darkest moment is just before the first rays of light. It is time to be all in for Jesus. He will use you to the degree of your surrender. The ministering angels are awaiting the Father's command as your words agree with Heaven's will for you.

"Are they not all ministering spirits, sent to render service for the sake of those who will inherit salvation?"
Hebrews 1:14

God is sending the angels to help us get this thing done. We need help from the muscle of Heaven, who do His will, and strengthen us in our heavenly endeavors. I was praying today:

My Father, expose the darkness! His reply was, "I am doing this right now!"

Light exposes darkness. Corruption must come to light and be shouted from the housetops revealing every hidden thing of evil. It cannot remain hidden. Jesus told Nicodemus in John Chapter 3 that evil men would not come to the light lest their evil deeds would be exposed, because light makes manifest and illuminates. These are the beginning of days that are called 'Golden Global Glory' as the move of the Father's heart is manifested on earth. The gross darkness can't conceal the Glory but must give way now to the light. This is the triggering of the 3rd Great Awakening and the Harvest. Samuel's are arising. That is why the battle is so fierce at this time. Can you hear the Spirit saying:

"Prepare, prepare, prepare. Get ready, Get ready!"

The force of Harp and Bowl Worship brings God's order to the chaos here on Earth. The harp represents instruments of praise, and the bowl represents the intercession furnace which burns. Look at Revelation 5:8..

"And when He (Jesus) had taken the book, the four living creatures and the twenty-four elders fell down before the Lamb, having each one a harp, and golden bowls of incense, which are the prayers of the saints."

When these two powerful forces are released in unison, tremendous energy is produced which unleashes the power of Heaven on the Earth to get things done. There is so much resistance here below, that we need supernatural help to accomplish God's will. Total surrender and cooperation with the Holy Spirit, allows us to tap into the release of Heaven's Worship. Things here in this fallen realm begin to change and shift as darkness bends the knee to the light. The sun of God's Love is radiating to shape the receding shadows which once engulfed us and blocked the light. The "bowl" is pictured here like a large golden bowl tipping back and forth until it overflows and releases cascades of prayers that have been prayed and stored up in this giant container in Heaven. As answers to prayers are poured out we experience breakthrough and glory on Earth.

This phenomena is increasing exponentially in recent months during this world-wide shut-down. What began experimentally, and rarely 30 years ago, has become a new wave and a movement in the Earth. This new move referred to as Prayer Rooms are springing up everywhere. God is authoring this power-house release of authority to spring forth now mightily. You might be familiar with this recent Facebook meme which circulated during the beginnings of the shut-down during the early months of 2020. There is a picture of planet Earth with the devil on one side and Father God on the other. Satan says to God, "See I've closed every church on the earth." The Father replies, "No, on the contrary, I've opened a church in every living room!" Checkmate! God always has the final move because it is His chess board. And it is God's chess pieces. In God's infinite wisdom He allows us the power of choice, but at the same time frustrates all the plans of the enemy. Remember the resurrection of the Son of God from satan's prison house, just when the demons were celebrating Christ's death, thinking they had won. All of hell cringed as the Spirit of God came into Jesus dead body as He arose and led captivity captive. Hallelujah!

God is picking a fight with the devil. He is using you and I to prove the enemy is a defeated foe. Our part is to...

"Submit yourselves, therefore, to God; resist the devil and he will flee from you." (James 4:7)

This battle is totally rigged in our favor!

The greatest battle strategy being used by the Holy Spirit today is proliferation of Houses of Prayer in every city. These garner the forces of cooperation with Holy Spirit and each other, releasing powerful weapons of warfare upon the devil and his camp. The truth is, he is terrified by you and I who God is using in these days.

I was laughing so hard today I could hardly park my truck and trailer in my driveway. My wife came outside and said, "Ken, why is your truck all up in the yard sideways?" Jesus had just spoken to me and said, "Ken, the devil is afraid of the sounds coming from your instruments." And then He added, "he is afraid of you"! All of a sudden the lights came on for me, as I realized that it was no random circumstance which brought damage to 2 of my choicest guitars I use in Harp and Bowl Worship. My sound has been dangerous to darkness! Today I was using a borrowed instrument to create sounds from Heaven in a 2 hour prayer set. I am still laughing as I think of this word I received. I am laughing as I write these lines. I am now reminded of this scripture in Psalm 2:4…

"He who sits in the Heavens laughs because He sees that satan's work comes to nothing!" (Mine)

You see, it is an act of futility for the devil to vent all his fury to attempt to undo the works of the Father…he is destined to lose and be cast into the lake of fire which burns with fire and brimstone forever and forever.

All the while our Heavenly Father rejoices over us with singing....look at Zephaniah 3:17

"The Lord thy God in the midst of thee is mighty; He will save, He will rejoice over thee with joy: He will rest in His love, He will joy over thee with singing".

We win if we don't quit!

Take courage and realize that the great cloud of witnesses in the heavenly arena are cheering us on right now. Their race is done, they have laid the foundation, but we are now coming into the finishing gates of the final victory lap. The devil has overplayed his hand because he knows his end is near. Revelation 12:11b

" ...Woe to you inhabiters of the Earth and the sea! For the devil is come down to you, having great wrath , because he knows he has but a short time".

Beloved, "Look up for your redemption is near"…
the Father is eagerly waiting for the precious fruit
of the Earth, so that He may say to Jesus, the Son,
"Arise, go get your Bride!" The long awaited
time is at hand. Heaven's gate is swinging wide to
receive the fruit of the end-time harvest of souls.
There is a marriage supper table being set for a
time of celebration. Jesus is coming and His reward is with Him. The fire in His eyes is His love
for His Bride!

CHAPTER SEVEN

WORSHIP: A FORCE TO BE RECKONED WITH

*"Who is she who looks forth as the morning, fair
as the moon, clear as the sun, Awesome as an army
with banners?"*
Songs 6:10

At this time there is stirring; an awakening. It
is an awakening of love; the first love. The hearts
of men are yearning for the real. They have been
too long dissatisfied with what we have passed off
as Christianity, which has eclipsed the real Jesus.
Make no mistake. The pure power of Heavenly
Worship being released is truly a force to be reck-
oned with. All the powers of hell are being crushed
under the weight of the Chabod, the weighty Presence of God manifested as the Worshipers arise,
lost and reveling in pools of His Glory. We are
unafraid, bold and courageous, to go forth in the
power of Holy array.

I saw today in the news great crowds forming on the beaches of California, coming to the heavenly sounds of Worship. Souls were being awakened and baptized in the sea, as forgiveness and mercy reigns. The crowd is moving northward. And all across this land there is a rumbling as this phenomena of Worship is springing up in small and large cities, led by selfless servants of God who are giving themselves over to Jesus. There is a Prayer and Worship movement that is being inspired and breathed upon by the Lord of Heaven by His Holy Spirit. It is His final checkmate in this war over worship. And it is a war we do win!

My Prayer

I repent of my own ways and surrender my self under the mighty Hand of God who is lifting me up to be counted in this number. I repent for folks that are the prayer-less and care-less with the Word of God. I am now praying from the Holy Fire of the living God! I have re-enlisted in the Army of God, and am going forth throughout the Earth to stir up good will and proclaim Jesus as Lord every where the souls of my feet do tread. I am trampling underneath my feet, the enemy, who has for so long robbed me of every blessing of God. My God has never with held any Good thing from me. Why would He, seeing He delights in me. It is His good pleasure to give me the Kingdom. Who can stop His Love from being manifested to me in my life right now?

"Shall tribulation, or distress, or persecution, or famine, or nakedness or peril or sword? As it is written, for thy sake we are killed all the day long; we are counted as sheep for the slaughter. Nay, in all these things we are more than conquerors through Him that loved us. For I am persuaded that neither death, nor life, nor angels, nor principalities, nor powers, nor things present, nor things to come; neither height, nor depth nor any other creature, shall be able to separate us from the love of God that is in Christ Jesus our Lord."
ROMANS 8:35-39

Sign up on the dotted line, God wants you for His army band. The enlistment poster is right there in front of you. The big finger of God is pointing at you....Yes He wants you!

The sooner we get on board, the sooner we can

help Jesus get this thing wrapped up and move forward to the millennium …our rewards and assignments are awaiting us…what we do now qualifies us and determines our place in the next move of God…welcome to His Royal Army of Worshipers. The Lord is raising up again the Tabernacle of David.

Revelation 22:12-13

" And ,behold, I come quickly; and my reward is with me, to give every man according as his work shall be. I am Alpha and Omega, the beginning and the end, the first and the last."

Revelation 22: 16,22

" I Jesus have sent mine angel to testify unto you these things in the churches. I am the root and offspring of David, and the bright and morning star."

"Surely I come quickly Amen."

"Even so, come Lord Jesus…."

56546307R00036